A MAN ALONE

Alan Falconer

A Man Alone

MEDITATIONS ON THE SEVEN LAST WORDS
OF JESUS ON THE CROSS

Illustrated by Pauline McGrath

the columba press

This edition published 1994 by
the columba press
93 The Rise, Mount Merrion, Blackrock, Co Dublin

First edition 1987
Cover by Bill Bolger
Illustrations by Pauline McGrath
Origination by The Columba Press
Printed in Ireland by
Genprint Ltd, Dublin

ISBN 1 85607 096 4

The author and publisher gratefully acknowledge the permission of those listed in the notes for permission to use copyright materials.

Contents

Introduction

Some twenty-five years ago I had the privilege of spending Holy Week in Paris worshipping with members of the Russian Orthodox Church in Exile. In a small building, formerly belonging to the German Lutherans, this small group of expatriate Russians daily celebrated the events leading to Easter.

On Good and Holy Friday, the death of Jesus is remembered. During the worship, a coffin is carried in procession right round the outside of the building, with the whole community following behind. The coffin is finally carried into the church, and placed on a catafalque in the centre of the church. Jesus really is dead.

As this service reached its climax, with the finality of death symbolised by the coffin, a young woman burst out in uncontrollable sobbing. Nothing could assuage her grief. No-one could console her. Throughout that day and the next she sobbed her heart out.

Christ her bridegroom had died.

Twenty-five years after the event, I am still unable to communicate the joy and liberation which exuded from her at the rising of Jesus on Easter Day. She radiated joy and gladness. Her life was transformed from that of mourning to one of continual thanksgiving. In everything she gave thanks to God for all his gifts – especially the gift of Jesus.

The central point of our faith rests on the death and rising of Jesus. If one looks at the New Testament, it is obvious that the earliest church lived in the light of the death and rising of Jesus. The earliest confessions of faith and hymns took this as their central theme. Such has been the case for the Church down through the ages.

Similarly in art – the death and rising of Jesus has been the subject of poetry from Ephraim of Syria to T. S. Eliot, the subject of art – da Vinci, Rembrandt, Grünewald, the subject of music – Theile, Sebastioni, Schütz, J. S. Bach to Frank Martin. Through these media of art we are invited to undertake the journey to the Cross and the Resurrection.

Few have managed to convey this so succinctly as J. S. Bach. In his famous B minor Mass, in his setting of the Creed, Bach sets *crucifixus* in dark colours, full of sustained long notes sung by the basses, an intensity which is both languid and full of sorrow; this is totally contrasted by the *Et Resurrexit*, a fast exciting piece, full of short notes sung by the sopranos, giving bright colours to the music, full of joy.

As with my Russian friend, and the earlier Christians, so with J. S. Bach, the thanksgiving, the joy, the fullness of hope only makes sense, only comes alive, because one has journeyed through the Passion. Without the Passion, with its tragedy, and hopelessness, there can be no Resurrection and no sense of Resurrection.

Unfortunately in today's Church life, it is too easy not

A MAN ALONE

to journey to Golgotha. With the pressure of life experienced today, it is too easy to attend church on Sundays, but feel it is too difficult to make it during the days of Holy Week. Understandable though this is, its effect is catastrophic. Too often we celebrate the joy and thanksgiving of Psalm Sunday one week, and the joy and thanksgiving of Easter Day the next week, and we fail personally or together to journey to Golgotha, without which neither makes sense. Yet our Holy Week worship does offer such an opportunity.

In the New Testament period itself, it looks as if the earliest Christians undertook the journey to the Cross in their worship. The gospel writers associate certain events as having happened at the 3rd, 6th or 9th hours. A number of New Testament scholars suggest convincingly that these hours represent the times of Jewish prayers – thus the Christians prayed about, and meditated upon, different parts of Christ's Passion in sequence, in prayer throughout Holy Week.

The churches today continue this contemplation of the Passion and Resurrection through prayer, reading, song and meditation.

One of the most powerful ways to undertake the journey of the Cross is to meditate on the Seven Last Words of Our Lord from the Cross. The Seven Last Words have played an important part in the devotions of our Churches. They have of course been set to music, above all by Joseph Haydn, and they have received prominent and eloquent treatment in the passion settings of Bach, Schülz and in the modern passion *Golgotha* by the Swiss composer, Frank Martin. They have become a traditional subject of meditation in some Anglican churches, and they form part of the Roman Catholic devotion, having arisen in the Middle Ages as one expression of the suffering of Jesus. In the Presbyterian hymnbook, they are the subject, one Word per hymn, of hymns nos. 244-250. In focusing on those words in prayer, then, we do so in company with Christians of every tradition.

The meditations on the Seven Last Words in this volume have been developed over a period of fifteen years. An invitation to conduct the Holy Week services for 1983 in the Sandymount Churches in Dublin provided an opportunity to work through the full cycle, and thus to share with Christian communities in their journey to the Cross. The context of these meditations is prayer, as Christians of different traditions strive to contemplate the centre of their faith.

These Words seem to me to convey the intensity and the anguish of this event, an event so powerful that men and women are still brought to new life, and are transformed into living the life of New Creation, in praising God in Jesus Christ through the Holy Spirit.

The invitation of this volume is well summed up by the French New Testament scholar, Etienne Trocme, in words which conclude his book *The Passion as Liturgy:*

Our understanding of the passion narrative is bound to become deeper if we join with the early Jerusalem Christians in their amazed contemplation of the sufferings and death of our common Lord, in their humble praise of God's saving act in Christ, in their assured hope of the resurrection of all believers.

In communion with Christians of all ages, and of all ecclesiastical traditions, let us therefore traverse the way of the Cross.

There were two others with him, criminals who were being led away to execution; and when they reached the place called The Skull, they crucified him there, and the criminals with him, one on his right, and the other on his left. Jesus said, 'Father, forgive them; they do not know what they are doing.'

They divided his clothes among them by casting lots. The people stood looking on, and their rulers jeered at him: 'He saved others: now let him save himself, if this is God's Messiah, his Chosen.' The soldiers joined in the mockery and came forward offering him their sour wine. 'If you are the king of the Jews,' they said, 'save yourself.' There was an inscription above his head which ran: 'This is the king of the Jews.'

Luke 23: 32-38

And so to the Cross The Accursed Hill

We nailed Him then
Aloft between the thieves, in the bright air,
The rabble and the readers mocked with oaths,
The hangman's squad were dicing for his clothes.
The two thieves jeered at him. Then it grew dark.
Till the noon sun was dwindled to a spark
And one by one the mocking mouths fell still.
We were alone on the accursed hill.
And we were still, not even the dice clicked,
Only the heavy blood-gouts dropped and ticked
On to the stone; the hill is all bald stone.
And now and then the hangers gave a groan.
Up in the dark, three shapes with arms outspread.
The blood-drops spat to show how slow they bled.
They rose up black against the ghastly sky.

John Masefield

And so to the Cross The Accused Hill

He humbled himself and became obedient unto death,
even the death of the cross.

Philippians 2:8

The man alone
Rejected by his disciples,
the men in whom he had placed trust.
The price had been too high for them.

Rejected by the political authorities;
it was better for one man to die
than for civil war to break out.
It was expedient for one man to die;
Roman justice after all
was only for her citizens.

Rejected by the religious authorities.
This man was dangerous.
He challenged traditions that had been cherished for generations,
that had made life comfortable,
free from facing up to the contemporary situation.

Rejected by his fellow countrymen.
Their expectations of political freedom
and a higher standard of living
had been dashed.

The signs of the Kingdom had been misread
or not considered at all.
It was easier to reject than to accept the challenge.

And so to the Cross The Accursed Hill

In the passion Jesus is a rejected Messiah. His rejection
robs the passion of its halo of glory … Suffering and rejection sum up the whole cross of Jesus. To die on the
cross means to die despised and rejected of men.

Dietrich Bonhoeffer

And so to the Cross The Accursed Hill

Father, forgive …
as at the end so from the very beginning of his ministry
Jesus preaches forgiveness
giving people – men and women, lost and hopeless –
the possibility of new life
free from their pasts to live life in the present
and for the future
free from the burden of guilt, able to be in right rela-
tion to God and other people.

Father, forgive …
as at the end so from the very beginning of his ministry
Jesus teaches forgiveness
– showing its importance for worship
If when you are bringing your gift to the altar,
go, first make peace with your brother
first, forgive then come and offer your gift.
– showing its importance for living
all of us in need of forgiveness
whoever is without sin, let them cast the first stone
– showing its importance for loving
the son said to his Father
'Father I have sinned against heaven and against you.

I no longer deserve to be called your son'
the Father said
'We are going to have a feast,
this son of mine was dead
and has come back to life'.

Jesus – the man alone
– a man deserted by and alienated from his family, and
community, his religious authorities and disciples, his
executioners and those others crucified.
– the man alone.

Jesus – the man enduring intense suffering
his hands, carpenter's hands,
hands that had touched the leper,
and blessed the children
these hands were twisted and splintered by the nails.

Jesus – the man alone
the man enduring intense suffering
his whole body stretched like a bow – taut,
so taut as to make movement impossible
struggling for breath.

Jesus – the man alone
the man enduring intense suffering
this man cries
Father, forgive them.
They do not know what they are doing.

Father, forgive
Father,
the special word used by Jesus for his God
Abba, Daddy –
the closest possible relationship
drawing men and women
to the Father through himself
in the midst of this intense suffering, Jesus cries.
Father, forgive ...

Jesus – the man alone
– the man who throughout his life preached forgiveness
giving folk the possibility of new life
– the man who throughout his life
taught the importance of forgiveness
for true worship, for true life, for true love
– this man in the midst of intense suffering
in the agony of despair and rejection
this man
who had preached and taught forgiveness
as at the beginning of his ministry so at the end
he lives forgiveness
showing forth true worship, true life, true love
this man
lives forgiveness
giving us the possibility of true worship,
true life,
true love.
Father, forgive them.
Father,
forgive
us.

FATHER, FORGIVE THEM

Men go to God when they are sore bestead,
Pray to him for succour, for his peace, for bread,
For mercy for them sick, sinning, or dead;
All men do so, Christian and unbelieving.

Men go to God when he is sore bestead,
Find him poor and scorned, without shelter or bread,
Whelmed under weight of the wicked, the weak, the
dead; Christians stand by God in his hour of grieving.

God goes to every man when sore bestead,
Feeds body and spirit with his bread;
For Christians, pagans alike he hangs dead,
And both alike forgiving

Dietrich Bonhoeffer

Man does not suffer that a world may be one; he does not suffer, even, that the will of God may be accomplished. He is, in fact, in the deepest suffering, evacuated of all real purpose at all. He is not suffering 'in order that'. His anguish does not allow him to be carried beyond the fact of suffering. And this is true so that the truth of suffering, its value as sign, may shine forth. But only for the few who are ready to read such a sign. Achievement, great moments, visible accomplishments, always have about them so much danger of distraction, egoism, ambiguity. But the sufferer who believes and takes his stand, not precisely on his suffering, not on the quality of his faith, not on the 'good' he is doing, nor on the response of his friends, but on Christ alone; which is to say, on the living truth of things – this man, perhaps for the first time, has become a true sign. He is the sign of the cross. There is quite possibly no other in the world today.

Daniel Berrigan

Prayer

Father in heaven, look down from your eternal throne:
Father of love, listen to your Son, your only Son,
praying for sinners,
for your children.
We have fallen deeply,
We have sinned greatly,
but your Son shed his blood
for our salvation,
for each one of us.
The blood of the Lamb does not call out for vengeance;
it wipes out sin.
Father of love, grant us grace,
listen to your Son,
O Father, listen to your Son.

In the course of his journey to Jerusalem, he was travelling through the borderlands of Samaria and Galilee. As he was entering a village he was met by ten men with leprosy. They stood some way off and called out to him, 'Jesus, Master, take pity on us.' When he saw them he said, 'Go and show yourselves to the priests'; and while they were on their way, they were made clean. One of them, finding himself cured, turned back praising God aloud. He threw himself down at Jesus's feet and thanked him. And he was a Samaritan. At this Jesus said: 'Were not all ten cleansed? The other nine, where are they? Could none be found to come back and give praise to God except this foreigner?' And he said to the man, 'Stand up and go on your way; your faith has cured you'.

Luke 17:11-19

A MAN ALONE

They divided his clothes among them by casting lots. The people stood looking on, and their rulers jeered at him: 'He saved others: now let him save himself, if this is God's Messiah, his Chosen.' The soldiers joined in the mockery and came forward offering him their sour wine. 'If you are the king of the Jews,' they said, 'save yourself.' There was an inscription above his head which ran: 'This is the king of the Jews.'

One of the criminals who hung there with him taunted him: 'Are not you the Messiah? Save yourself, and us.' But the other rebuked him: 'Have you no fear of God? You are under the same sentence as he. For us it is plain justice; we are paying the price for our misdeeds; but this man has done nothing wrong.' And he said, 'Jesus, remember me when you come to your throne.' He answered, 'I tell you this: today you shall be with me in paradise.'

Luke 23:35-43

Jesus, the man alone
abandoned by his disciples and friends
rejected by the religious authorities as too dangerous
making life uncomfortable by his questions
challenging long established customs
inviting people to relate to God directly
rejected by the political authorities
as a disturber of the peace
upsetting the equilibrium of Roman-Jewish relations
a harmless simple man
yet subverting the 'peace' of society
rejected by his fellow citizens as a failure
for not fulfilling their political expectations
not satisfying their search for
higher economic standards
the man alone –
this man
whose bones are crushed by nails
whose body is held taut by its position
pinioned on wood
this man
asks his Father to forgive them.

Jesus, the man alone –

In the passion Jesus is a rejected Messiah … To die on
the Cross means to die despised and rejected of men.
Dietrich Bonhoeffer

A MAN ALONE

Jesus
despised and rejected by men and women
in intense agony and despair
is jeered and mocked at by the crowd
He saved others - let him save himself ...
If you're a king save yourself ...
Work your miracles now ...
Get off the Cross ...

Jesus – the man alone
hanged between two criminals
between two men whose attitudes, values
were so opposed to those of himself
they had accepted conflict as the method of redress
for personal or national or group disabilities
they had embraced violence and hatred
as part of their code
such a man hears Jesus
Father, forgive them ...
the words pierce him
strange words
– a benediction on those who had tormented,
disgraced and killed this man Jesus
– an all-pervading love which could solicit forgiveness
for the evil-doers
in this he sees the superiority of the Way of the Cross
over the way of conflict – his way up to that time
the words pierce him
strange words
– words of love and hope
and so he surrenders to Jesus
Jesus, remember me
when you come into your kingdom

TODAY YOU WILL BE WITH ME ...   27

Jesus, remember me
Jesus
called by his name
only once before that had happened to him
travelling in Galilee, as he entered a village
ten lepers came to meet him,
'Jesus, take pity on us
Jesus make us whole
give us the possibility of fullness of life'
ten lepers cured
having newness of life

Jesus
despised and rejected by men and women
in intense agony and despair
rejected

To be rejected is a higher degree of suffering. Suffering
can be borne with dignity. One must have compassion
for the suffering. In an unjust world, they say, 'the just
man shall suffer much.' But one who is rejected cannot
be a prophet and a just man – he is rejected in God's
name as Godless, in the name of the holy law as a law-
breaker. Rejection robs this suffering man of every dignity. His suffering has no honour.

Jürgen Moltmann

Jesus
in intense agony
despised and rejected
fighting for breath
taunted, abused, mocked ...
In the midst of this
the vilest of experiences
one of those hanged with him joins in the derision

Jesus – the man alone
hanged between two criminals
they may have been patriots,
nationalist rebels who could not bear the tyranny
and injustice of Roman rule
or socially and economically disadvantaged persons
who had become bitter against the privileged groups
– the absentee landlords who drained the country of
the resources
– the Roman invaders who exploited by securing the
best jobs for themselves and their friends
or anti-religious – disillusioned by the contrast
between the outward pomp and trimmings of
organised religion and its inward emptiness
condemned as blasphemers
or just plan thieves, cowards,
men who had violated the laws of society because they
didn't have the stamina and guts to observe the law
and face life
two criminals
one of whom joins in the mocking

Jesus
called by his name
a criminal, touched and pierced
 by his words of forgiveness
asks to be included
to be given the possibility of new life
of wholeness

Jesus
the man alone –
in the midst of the clamour of abuse and insult
in the midst of the intense suffering and agony
in the midst of the rejection and the despair
gives the possibility of new life through his love
gives the possibility of wholeness, of holiness
to one who responds
'Today you will be with me in paradise'

Jesus
the man alone –
'in the act of dying he brings the liberating reign of
God into the situation of deepest abandonment'
Today you will he with me, as at the Garden of Eden
in the fullest relationship with God
in a relationship of wholeness
the destiny of those made and sustained
in the image of God

Jesus
the man alone –
in intense agony and despair
this man makes whole –
holy by his love and forgiveness

Today
you will be with me in paradise

'Would you know your Lord's meaning in this? Learn it well. Love was his meaning. Who showed it to you? Love. What did he show you? Love. Why did he show you? For love. Hold fast to this, and you shall learn and know more about love, but you will never need to know or understand about anything else for ever and ever.' Thus did I learn that love was our Lord's meaning.

Julian of Norwich

Upon the Ensignes of Christes Crucifyinge

O sweete and bitter monuments of paine,
Bitter to Christ who all the paine endur'd,
But sweete to mee, whose Death my life procur'd,
How shall I full express, such loss, such gaine.
My tongue shall bee my Penne, mine eyes shall raine
Teares for my Inke, the Cross where I was cur'd
Shall be my Booke, where having all abjur'd
And calling heavens to record in that plaine
Thus plainely will I write: no sinne like mine.
When I have done, doe thou Jesu divine
Take up the tarte Spunge of thy Passion
And blot it forth: then bee thy spirit the Quill,
Thy bloode the Inke, and with compassion
Write thus upon my soule: thy Jesu still.

William Alabaster

Prayer

Lamb of God, you are the mediator
of complete mercy, grace and love.
The repentant sinner barely has to call out
'Think of me, when you come into your kingdom,'
before you promise him so generously
'Today you will be with me in paradise.'
Lord and God,
look at us;
see our true repentance at the foot of the cross,
and, at the hour of our death,
give us this same consolation:
'Today you will be with me in paradise.'

Three days later there was a wedding at Cana in Galilee. The mother of Jesus was there, and Jesus and his disciples had also been invited. When they ran out of wine, since the wine provided for the wedding was all finished, the mother of Jesus said to him, 'They have no wine' Jesus said, 'Woman, why turn to me? My hour has not come yet.' His mother said to the servants, 'Do whatever he tells you.' There were six stone water jars standing there, meant for the ablutions that are customary among the Jews: each could hold twenty or thirty gallons. Jesus said to the servants, 'Fill the jars with water,' and they filled them to the brim. 'Draw some out now,' he told them, 'and take it to the steward.' They did this; the steward tasted the water, and it had turned into wine. Having no idea where it came from – only the servants who had drawn the water knew – the steward called the bridegroom and said, 'People generally serve the best wine first, and keep the cheaper sort till the guests have had plenty to drink, but you have kept the best wine till now.'

This was the first of the signs given by Jesus; it was given at Cana in Galilee. He let his glory be seen, and his disciples believed in him. After this he went down to Capernaum with his mother and the brothers, but they stayed there only a few days.

John 2:1-12

A MAN ALONE

Near the cross of Jesus stood his mother and his mother's sister, Mary the wife of Clopas, and Mary of Magdala. Seeing his mother and the disciple he loved standing near her, Jesus said to his mother, 'Woman, this is your son.' Then to the disciple he said, 'This is your mother.' And from that moment the disciple made a place for her in his home.

John 19:25-27

WOMAN, BEHOLD YOUR SON

Jesus
abandoned and rejected by friends and disciples
rejected by the religious authorities
crucified by the political power
despised by his fellow citizens as a false prophet
suffering intense physical pain
his bones crushed
his body pinioned
struggling for breath
lives forgiveness
giving human beings the possibility of true worship
true life
true love
makes people whole
sharing holiness through his love and forgiveness.

Jesus
the man alone
seeing his mother
in the midst of the mocking and jeering
cries
Woman, this is your son

What a wedding feast this is –
that he calls her 'Woman' once more
What a wedding this is –
her Son hanging on a gibbet between two criminals
– yet alone

Three years earlier
he wasn't alone then
along with family and friends
he celebrated the wedding of a friend
joyfully joining in their celebration

at the prospect of new life
– the creation of a new family
new creation
new life
new relationship

     Three years earlier
he wasn't alone then
he had acted at the behest of his mother
though the 'hour' had not yet come
– the hour of fulfillment
when God's promise of deliverance
of liberation
– symbolised in the abundance of wine
is at hand
the hour of new creation
new life
new relationship

     Three years earlier
he wasn't alone then
he transformed that celebration
water into wine
the water of purification
the water of baptism
into wine – symbol of Messianic deliverance
the wine of life
new creation
new life
new relationship
true creation
true life
true relationship

Three years earlier
he wasn't alone then
he had said Woman,
Woman, what have you to do with me?
indicative of new relationship
no longer would human ties and obligations
influence his actions in any way
the event of revelation
is independent of human desires
and cannot forcibly be brought about
by human supplication
it comes to pass where and how God wills
surpassing all human expectations

At the wedding feast
three years earlier
the genuine Bridegroom comes
to a private festival of marriage
and utterly transforms it
a new family is born – a new creation
water becomes wine – a new life
a mother becomes 'Woman' – a new relationship
What a wedding feast this is
that he calls her 'Woman' once more

What a wedding this is
her son hanging on a gibbet between two criminals
– yet alone.

At this wedding feast
the bridegroom once again
transforms.
'Woman, this is your Son'

no longer are blood ties the most important
the ties of relationship
are predominantly those in and through Jesus Christ
the new relationship of this wedding feast
is love for each other in and through Jesus
– a relationship of joy and oneness
in fully responding to God
in being fully attentive to each other

At this wedding feast
the bridegroom once again
transforms.
'Woman, this is your Son'
a new creation is born
the family of all human beings
striving together
to create a world in which
forgiveness and love predominate
– a world of peace
where each person has and grants to the other –
the space and the time to live

At this wedding feast
the bridegroom once again
transforms.
'Woman, this is your son'
A new life of freedom
of truth
of joy
begins here
with him – who is the Way, the Truth and the Life

Jesus
– the man alone
suffering and rejected
in his very living a life of forgiveness and love transforms this suffering
into the wedding feast
– of new creation
new relationship
new life
– of true creation
true relationship
true life

Jesus – the man alone
Woman, this is your Son

Jesus and his Mother

My only son, more God's than mine,
Stay in this garden ripe with pears.
The yielding of their substance wears
A modest and contented shine:
And when they weep with age, not brine
But lazy syrup are their tears.
'I am my own and not my own.'

He seemed much like another man,
That silent foreigner who trod
Outside my door with lily rod:
How could I know what I began
Meeting the eyes more furious than
The eyes of Joseph, those of God?
I was my own and not my own.

And who are these twelve labouring men?
I do not understand your words:
I taught you speech, we named the birds,
You marked their big migrations then
Like any child. So turn again
To silence from the place of crowds.
'I am my own and not my own.'

Why are you sullen when I speak?
Here are your tools, the saw and knife
And hammer on your bench. Your life
Is measured here in week and week
Planed as the furniture you make,
And I will teach you like a wife
To be my own and all my own.

Who like an arrogant wind blown
Where he may please, needs no content?
Yet I remember how you went
To speak with scholars in furred gown.
I hear an outcry in the town;
Who carried that dark instrument?
'One all his own and not his own.'

Treading the green and nimble sward
I stare at a strange shadow thrown.
Are you the boy I bore alone,
No doctor near to cut the cord?
I cannot reach to call you Lord,
Answer me as my only son.
'I am my own and not my own.'

Thom Gunn

A MAN ALONE

Give me to recognise in other men, Lord God, the radiance of your own face. The irresistible light of your eyes, shining in the depths of things, has already driven me into undertaking the work I had to do and facing the difficulties I had to overcome: grant me now to see you also and above all in the most inward, most perfect, most remote levels of the souls of my brother-men.

The gift you ask of me for these brothers of mine - the only gift my heart can give them - is not the overflowing tenderness of those special preferential loves which you implant in our lives as the most powerful created agent of our inward growth: it is something less tender but just as real and of even greater strength. Your will is that, with the help of your Eucharist, between men and my bother-men there should be revealed that basic attraction (already dimly felt in every love once it becomes strong) which mystically transforms the myriads of rational creatures into (as it were) a single monad in you, Christ Jesus.

Teilhard de Chardin

Prayer

Jesus, your mother stood desolate
weeping and sighing by the Cross,
bearing the agony of your suffering
seven times over in her own being
hardly able to contain herself
and yet steadfast and calm.
She took the faithful disciple as her son,
and showed us true discipleship,
by being obedient to your call to accept others fully.
Strengthen us,
as we try to be steadfast and faithful to your call
to initiate a new creation.

My God, my God, why hast
thou forsaken me
and art so far from saving me,
from heeding my groans?

O my God, I cry in the day-time
but thou dost not answer,
in the night I cry but get no respite.

And yet thou art enthroned in holiness,
thou art he whose praises Israel sings.

In thee our fathers put their trust;
they trusted, and thou didst rescue them.

Unto thee they cried and were delivered;
in thee they trusted and were not put to shame.

But I am a worm, not a man,
abused by all men, scorned by the people.

All who see me jeer at me,
make mouths at me and wag their heads:

'He threw himself on the Lord for rescue;
let the Lord deliver him, for he holds him dear!'

Psalm 22:1-8

At midday a darkness tell over the whole land, which lasted till three in the afternoon; and at three Jesus cried aloud, 'Eli, Eli, lama sabachthani?', which means, 'My God, my God, why hast thou forsaken me?'

Mark 15:33-34

The man alone
Jesus
alienated from his own people
an embarrassment to his family
– his home town had found him presumptuous
and laughed him to scorn
– the carpenter's son
the son of those good folk, Mary and Joseph,
acclaimed as a prophet

Jesus – a man alone
alienated from his family and his community
the religious authorities felt threatened
by his complete openness
to people who were affluent and powerful
to people who were oppressed
to people who were socially unacceptable
the Law regulated relationships and behaviour,
for the religious,
not the disposition of openness

Jesus – a man alone
to the crowds who had listened to him on the way
his words were so costly and so difficult
– words perceived as Words of Judgement
rather than Words of Liberation
and so, ultimately, they rejected him

Jesus – a man alone
his own inner circle of friends
his disciples
they too had melted away
one had connived to have him tried

one had been faithful
– but when recognised, blind panic struck
he, too, melted away

    Jesus – a man alone
a complete stranger had to be pressed into service
to carry his cross
even his executioners had been foreigners
– they spoke a different language
the two men crucified with him
their lives, a total denial
of all that he had lived and taught

    Jesus – a man alone
– a man enduring intense suffering

It is infinitely easier to suffer in obedience to a human command that to accept suffering as free, responsible men. It is infinitely easier to suffer as public heroes, to suffer physical death, than to endure spiritual suffering. Christ suffered as a free man alone, apart and in ignominy, in body and spirit ...

Dietrich Bonhoeffer

    Jesus – a man alone
a man enduring intense suffering
the emptiness of affliction

Affliction is something specific and impossible to describe in any other terms ... Affliction constrained Christ to implore that he might be spared; to seek consolation from man; to believe he was forsaken by the Father. It forced a just man to cry out against God ... This is no blasphemy but a genuine cry of anguish ... Affliction makes God appear to be absent for a time, more absent than a dead man, more absent than light in the utter darkness of a cell. A kind of horror submerges the whole soul ... The soul has to go on loving in the emptiness, or at least to go on wanting to love ...

Simone Weil

God creates everything out of nothing, and everything which God is to use he first reduces to nothing.

Soren Kierkegaard

Jesus – a man alone
a man enduring intense suffering
a man experiencing the emptiness of affliction
the utmost despair
a man reduced to nothing
this man cries
My God, my God, why have you forsaken me?

Jesus
– entering into the depths of the desolating experience
the experience of the 'righteous sufferers'
the whole range of human emotions
from near despair
to confidence that even yet
God will help in this time of trouble

Jesus – a man alone
a man enduring intense suffering
a man experiencing the emptiness of affliction
the utmost despair
a man reduced to nothing
the man who associated himself with the anguish
of the 'righteous sufferers'
for this man
this cry
was a cry of
absolute
dereliction
My God, my God, why have you forsaken me?
Eloi, Eloi, lama Sabachthani?

Having Confessed

Having confessed he feels
That he should go down on his knees and pray
For forgiveness for his pride, for having
Dared to view his soul from the outside.
Lie at the heart of the emotion, time
Has its own work to do. We must not anticipate
Or awaken for a moment. God cannot catch us
Unless we stay in the unconscious room
Of our hearts. We must be nothing,
Nothing that God may make us something.
We must not touch the immortal material
We must not daydream tomorrow's judgement –
God must be allowed to surprise us.
We have sinned, sinned like Lucifer
By this anticipation. Let us lie down again
Deep in anonymous humility and God
May find us worthy material for His hand.

Patrick Kavanagh

Alone, alone, about a dreadful wood
Of conscious evil runs a lost mankind,
Dreading to find its Father lest it find
The Goodness it has dreaded is not good:
Alone, alone, about our dreadful wood.

Where is that Law for which we broke our own,
Where now that Justice for which Flesh resigned
Her hereditary right to passion, Mind
His will to absolute power? Gone. Gone.
Where is that Law for which we broke our own?

The Pilgrim Way has led to the Abyss.
Was it to meet such grinning evidence
We left our richly odoured ignorance?
Was the triumphant answer to be this?
The Pilgrim Way has led to the Abyss.

We who must die demand a miracle.
How could the Eternal do a temporal act,
The Infinite become a finite fact?
Nothing can save us that is possible:
We who must die demand a miracle.

W. H. Auden

Prayer

Why have you abondoned me?
Who can see here any trace of the divine?
Who can fathom this mystery?
O God of strength and power and might,
we are the work of your hands,
and it is your love that has redeemed us.
Lord, we thank you with all our hearts.
For us you suffered pain and mockery,
Abandonment, anguish and agony.
Lord, who could tail to love you?
Who could grieve you by sinning?
Who could not acknowledge your graciousness?
Nothing, no nothing shall separate us from you,
Now, or in all eternity.

He had to pass through Samaria, and on his way came to a Samaritan town called Sychar, near the plot of ground which Jacob gave to his son Joseph and the spring called Jacob's well. It was about noon, and Jesus, tired after his journey, sat down by the well.

The disciples had gone away to the town to buy food. Meanwhile a Samaritan woman came to draw water. Jesus said to her, 'Give me a drink.' The Samaritan woman said, 'What! You a Jew, ask a drink of me, a Samaritan woman?' (Jews and Samaritans, it should be noted, do not use vessels in common). Jesus answered her, 'If only you knew what God gives, and who it is that is asking you for a drink, you would have asked him and he would have given you living water.' 'Sir,' the woman said, you have no bucket and this well is deep. How can you give me "living water"? Are you a greater man than Jacob our ancestor, who gave us the well, and drank from it himself, he and his sons, and his cattle too?' Jesus said, 'Everyone who drinks this water will be thirsty again, but whoever drinks the water that I shall give him will never suffer thirst any more. The water that I shall give him will be an inner spring always welling up for eternal life.' 'Sir,' said the woman, 'give me that water, and then I shall not be thirsty, nor have to come all this way to draw.'

John 4:4-15

After that, Jesus, aware that all had now come to its appointed end, said in fulfilment of scripture, 'I thirst.' A jar stood there full of sour wine; so they soaked a sponge with the wine, fixed it on a javelin, and held it up to his lips.

John 19:28-29

Jesus – the man alone
deserted by and alienated from
his family and community
the religious authorities
the disciples – his inner circle of friends
alien to his executioners
and the men crucified alongside him

Jesus – the man alone
the man enduring intense suffering,
who took suffering upon himself freely,
suffering alone
apart
and in ignominy
in body and spirit

Jesus – the man alone
experiencing the emptiness of affliction
the utmost despair
experiencing the absence of God
an absence more real and devastating
than the absence of light
in the utter darkness of a cell
emptiness
nothingness

Jesus – the man alone
entering the depths of a desolating experience
cries
My God, my God, why have you forsaken me?

What agony
in the tension of despair, his mouth dries up
in the tension of the sheer physical pain,
his tongue cleaves to the roof of his mouth
no moisture
nothing to swallow but his own despair and loneliness
his throat dries up
his face becomes taut and full of the unspoken anguish
finally, with a superhuman effort, he cries 'I thirst'
and immediately a soldier gives him something
to quench that thirst
– a sponge soaked in vinegar, on the end of a hyssop
stick, was put to his mouth

This event took place
at the sixth hour on that fateful day

He had to pass through Samaria, and on his way came
to a Samaritan town called Sychar, near the plot of
ground which Jacob gave to his son Joseph and the
spring called Jacob's well. It was about noon, and
Jesus, tired after his journey, sat down by the well. The
disciples had gone away to the town to buy food.
Meanwhile a Samaritan woman came to draw water.
Jesus said to her 'Give me a drink.'

It was about the sixth hour.
At Sychar,
Jesus receives water from a Samaritan woman
– Samaritan and Jew had absolutely no contact
 with each other.
At Golgotha, Jesus receives vinegar
from a Roman soldier
– Roman and Jew had as little contact with each other
as possible

Anyone who drinks the water that I shall give
will never be thirsty again

　　I thirst
total identification with us

　　It was about the sixth hour
to the agony of the physical suffering
to the agony of despair and nothingness
to the agony of total isolation from all people
was added the agony of thirst, caused by these things
and contributed to by the heat

　　I thirst
this is a man hanging on this gibbet
not a scapegoat, as Pilate wanted
not a religious crank,
as the religious authorities wanted
not an ideal,
as men and women of all ages have wanted
it is a man who cries 'I thirst'
who remembers the Woman by the Well
– the living water
and now he is parched

---

who remembers asking the Sons of Zebedee
if they could drink the Cup of which he must drink
the Cup of Love
the Cup of Obedience
and now he is parched
who remembers the Cup
which he preferred not to have
but he embraces it
and now he is parched

The man alone
parched
taut
in agony
relieved by vinegar on a hyssop stick
'for my thirst they gave me vinegar to drink'
– one with the parched condition
of the righteous sufferers

Jesus – the man alone – says
Everyone who drinks this water will be thirsty again,
but whoever drinks the water that I shall give him
will never suffer thirst any more.
The water that I shall give him
will be an inner spring
always welling up for eternal life

Jesus – the man alone – asks us
if we can drink the cup that he drank of
– the cup which he offers us

Jesus – the man alone – says
I thirst

I THIRST

When my son saw me under the cross and noticed his mourning friends he cried out to his heavenly father, with a loud and wailing voice: 'My father, why have you forsaken me?' It was as if he wanted to say: 'Nobody except you can have mercy upon me'.

The look in his eyes seemed to us already half faded away, his teeth smeared with blood, his face cruelly distorted, his mouth open and his saliva mingled with blood. His body was hollow and dried out as if he had no longer any entrails. As all his blood had been lost, he turned pale. His members were convulsively stretched out, hair and beard encrusted with blood. When finally death came near, the heart of my son broke under the violence of pain. His body contracted, once again his head lifted and then fell forward on his breast. Yet his mouth remained open so that his tongue, smeared with blood, could be seen. His hands spasmodically gripped the nails and then released their grip. Arms and legs lost their tension and his body hung heavily on the cross.

Saint Bridget of Sweden

Batter my heart, three person'd God; for, you
As yet but knocke, breathe, shine, and seeke to mend;
That I may rise, and stand, o'erthrow mee, 'and bend
Your force, to breake, blowe, burn and make me new.
I, like an usurpt towne, to 'another due,
Labour to'admit you, but Oh, to no end,
Reason your viceroy in mee, mee should defend,
But is captiv'd, and proves weake or untrue.
Yet dearly'I love you, 'and would be loved faine,
But am betroth'd unto your enemie:
Divorce mee, 'untie, or break that knot againe,
Take mee to you, imprison mee, tor I
Except you'enthrall mee, never shall be free,
Nor ever chast, except you ravish mee.

John Donne

Prayer

O people, refrain from vengeance, calm your rage.
Be softened by compassion,
awaken mercy in your hearts.
Jesus calls: 'I thirst',
and he is offered wine mingled with gall.
Such is his refreshment.
Can cruelty go further?
He can no longer contain the pain
in his thirst before his death,
and they offered him gall.
Strengthen us,
that we may show mercy at all times.

After these words Jesus looked up to heaven and said: 'Father, the hour has come. Glorify thy Son, that the Son may glorify thee. For thou hast made him sovereign over all mankind, to give eternal life to all whom thou hast given him. This is eternal life: to know thee who alone art truly God, and Jesus Christ whom thou has sent.'

'I have glorified thee on earth by completing the work which thou gavest me to do; and now, Father, glorify me in thy own presence with the glory which I had with thee before the world began.'

'I have made thy name known to the men whom thou didst give me out of the world. They were thine, thou gavest them to me, and they have obeyed thy command. Now they know that all thy gifts have come to me from thee; for I have taught them all that I learned from thee, and they have received it: they know with certainty that I came from thee; they have had faith to believe that thou didst send me.'

'I pray for them; I am not praying for the world but for those whom thou hast given me, because they belong to thee. All that is mine is thine, and what is thine is mine; and through them has my glory shone.'

'I am to stay no longer in the world, but they are still in the world, and I am on my way to thee. Holy Father, protect by the power of thy name those whom thou hast given me.'

John 17:1-11

Having received the wine, he said, 'It is accomplished!'
He bowed his head and gave up his spirit.

John 19:30

Jesus
the man alone
abandoned and rejected by his friends and disciples
rejected by the political power
despised by his fellow citizens as a false prophet
feeling abandoned by God
his bones crushed
his body pinioned
struggling for breath
parched, thirsty, drained
transforming his suffering
into the wedding feast
of the new creation
new relationship
new life

Jesus
the man alone
yet the only man in control
each event
each decisive moment of the Passion
shaped by him
– the active subject of each verb – each action
in the Garden
approaching the cohort and asking
Who are you searching for?

In front of Caiaphas
taking the initiative
in confirming his preaching
before Pilate
refusing to answer Pilate's last question
in which he tried to exonerate Jesus

at the accursed hill
taking the initiative in forgiving
making whole, holy
establishing a new creation

Jesus
the man alone
yet the only man in control
and finally
the free agent of death
even at the moment of dying Jesus acts
he breathed his last
he yielded up his spirit

Jesus
the man alone
yet the only man in control
and finally
the free agent of death
the cross of agony
the cross of despair and rejection
yet the cross of victory

Tetelestai
it is finished
it is complete
it is fulfilled
it is finalised

Jesus
the man alone
chose the moment of death
by bowing his head
restricting his breathing
causing life to cease

Jesus
the man alone
yet the man in control
no need to break his legs
no need to hasten the end
so that the events of the Feast Day
could begin unsullied
it is finished
Jesus the man alone
chose the moment of death

Tetelestai
it is finished
the work he had been sent to do
to bring human beings into oneness with God
to bring human beings into oneness with each other
through forgiveness – generating new life
healing – generating wholeness – holiness
love – generating new relationships

Tetelestai
it is finished – a cry of joy, of victory
the work he had been sent to do
to celebrate the wedding feast
of new life
new creation
new relationship

Jesus
the man alone
yet the only man in control
it is finished
'I have glorified you on earth
and finished the work
that you gave me to do'

Jesus
the man alone
'keep those you have given me true to your name
so that they may be one as we are'

Jesus
the man alone
keep us true to your name
may we be one in you
– a new creation in you

The Killing

That was the day they killed the Son of God
On a squat hill-top by Jerusalem.
Zion was bare, her children from their maze
Sucked by the demon curiosity
Clean through the gates. The very halt and blind
Had somehow got themselves up to the hill.

After the ceremonial preparation,
The scourging, nailing, nailing against the wood,
Erection of the main-trees with their burden,
While from the hill rose an orchestral wailing,
They were there at last, high up in the soft spring day.
We watched the writhings, heard the moanings, saw
The three heads turning on their separate axles
Like broken wheels left spinning. Round his head
Was loosely bound a crown of plaited thorn
That hurt at random, stinging temple and brow
As the pain swung into its envious circle.
In front the wreath was gathered in a knot
That as he gazed looked like the last stump left
Of a death-wounded deer's great antlers. Some
Who came to stare grew silent as they looked,
Indignant or sorry. But the hardened old
And the hard-hearted young, although at odds
From the first morning, cursed him with one curse,
Having prayed for a Rabbi or an armed Messiah
And found the Son of God. What use to them
Was a God or a Son of God? Of what avail
For purposes such as theirs? Beside the cross-foot,
Alone, four women stood and did not move
All day. The sun revolved, the shadow wheeled,

The evening fell. His head lay on his breast,
But in his breast they watched his heart move on
By itself alone, accomplishing its journey.
Their taunts grew louder, sharpened by the knowledge
That he was walking in the park of death,
Far from their rage. Yet all grew stale at last,
Spite, curiosity, envy, hate itself.
They waited only for death and death was slow
And came so quietly they scarce could mark it.
They were angry then with death and death's deceit.

I was a stranger, could not read these people
Or this outlandish deity. Did a God
Indeed in dying cross my life that day
By chance, he on his road and I on mine?

Edwin Muir

This is the truth of the gospel, that the true disciples of Christ crucified should follow him with the cross. A great example has been shown, a great mystery has been declared; the Son of God willingly (for he was offered up because he himself willed it) mounted the cross as a criminal, leaving to us, as it is written, an example, that we should follow his footsteps. Blessed then is the man who becomes a sharer in this passion and this shame. For there is something wonderful there concealed; for the foolishness of God is wiser than men, and the weakness of God is stronger than men. Strangely is immeasurable wisdom discerned in foolishness, and in weakness incomparable strength. Thus are hidden there all choice consolations, the secrets of salvation; but they are difficult in order that they may be precious; they are veiled in order that they may be merited by few; merited indeed by few, since they too are wonderful. Therefore let us patiently bear all adversaries for truth's sake, that we may be sharers in the Lord's passions; for if we suffer together with him, together we shall reign.

Columban

Prayer

Fastened to the sacrificial wood,
Jesus hung, in darkness.
Then he cried aloud
'It is completed'.
The wrong done by that wood
will be made good by this man.
Woe to you, evil ones,
Woe to you who are blind,
Woe to all who heap sin upon sin.
Consider well, O men,
Will you be treated with mercy,
When he comes in his glory and power?
Save us, Redeemer, from damnation.
Hear us, son of God. Hear our cry.
Do not let your suffering and death
Leave us untouched.
Grant to us a future heaven
where we will rejoice with you forever.

Now it was the practice of his parents to go to Jerusalem every year for the Passover festival; and when he was twelve, they made the pilgrimage as usual. When the festive season was over and they started for home, the boy Jesus stayed behind in Jerusalem. His parents did not know of this; but thinking that he was with the party they journeyed on for a whole day, and only then did they begin looking for him among their friends and relations. As they could not find him, they returned to Jerusalem to look for him; and after three days they found him sitting in the temple surrounded by the teachers, listening to them and putting questions; and all who heard him were amazed at his intelligence and the answers he gave. His parents were astonished to see him there, and his mother said to him, 'My son, why have you treated us like this? Your father and I have been searching for you with great anxiety.' 'What made you search?' he said. 'Did you not know that I was bound to be in my Father's house?' But they did not understand what he meant.

Luke 2:41-50

By now it was about midday and a darkness fell over the whole land, which lasted until three in the afternoon; the sun's light failed. And the curtain of the temple was torn in two. Then Jesus gave a loud cry and said, 'Father, into thy hands I commit my spirit'; and with these words he died.

Luke 23:44-46

Jesus
the man alone
yet the only man in control
abandoned and rejected
despised
in intense agony
his bones crushed
body pinioned
struggling for breath
parched, thirsty, drained

Jesus
the man alone
yet the only man in control
transforms his suffering
into the wedding feast
the new creation
the new relationship
the new life
oneness of being in God
oneness with each other in Jesus
oneness signified in the water of baptism
sustained in the wine of the eucharist

Jesus
the man alone
yet the only man in control
completing his Father's work
ends his life
Father into your hands I commit my spirit

Jesus
the man alone
his final words pointing to his Father
abandoning himself to the Father
a triumphant proclamation of trust

Jesus
the man alone
his whole ministry
a paean of praise of God, the Father
do you not know that I must be busy
with my Father's business?

Jesus
the man alone
makes us partakers of his Spirit
enabling us to do the Father's business in him
enabling us to take our part
in the wedding feast of the new creation

Jesus
the man alone
the man for others
the man for us

Father into your hands I commit my spirit

And so the Cross   The Accursed Hill

Jesus made it clear beyond all doubt that the 'must' of
suffering applies to his disciples no less than to himself.
Just as Christ is Christ only in virtue of his suffering
and rejection, so the disciple is a disciple only insofar as
he shares his Lord's suffering and rejection and cruci-
fixion.

Dietrich Bonhoeffer

Are you willing to be sponged out, erased, cancelled,
made nothing?
Are you willing to be made nothing?
dipped into oblivion?
If not, you will never really change.
The phoenix renews her youth
only when she is burnt, burnt alive, burnt down
to hot and flocculent ash.
The small stirring of a new small bub in the nest
with strands of down like floating ash
shows that she is renewing her youth like the eagle,
Immortal bird.

D H Lawrence

And so the Cross   The Accursed Hill

The Cross transforms our lives. After this encounter,
our lives can never be the same. Our whole life is then
lived in the perspective of this suffering and rejection.
The Cross points in all directions. It is an invitation – a
costly invitation – to all men and women.

I suppose
    that at first, it was people who invented borders,
and then borders
    started to invent people.
It was borders who invented police,
    armies and border guards.
It was borders who invented
customs-men, passports, and other shit.
Thank God,
    we have invisible threads and threadlets,
born of the threads of blood
    from the nails in the palms of Christ.
These threads struggle through,
    tearing apart the barbed wire,
leading love to join love
    and anguish to unite with anguish.

Yevgeny Yertushenko

Ecce Homo

Whose is this horrifying face,
This putrid flesh, discoloured, flayed,
Fed on by flies, scorched by the sun?
Whose are these hollow red-filmed eyes
And thorn-spiked head and spear-stuck side?
Behold the Man: He is Man's Son.

Forget the legend, tear the decent veil
That cowardice or interest devised
To make their mortal enemy a friend,
To hide the bitter truth all His wounds tell,
Lest the great scandal be no more disguised:
He is in agony till the world's end.

And we must never sleep during this time!
He is suspended on the cross-tree now
And we are onlookers at the crime,
Callous contemporaries of the slow
Torture of God. Here is the hill
Made ghastly by His spattered blood.

Whereon He hangs and suffers still:
See, the centurions wearing riding-boots,
Black shirts and badges and peaked caps,
Greet one another with raised-arm salutes;
They have cold eyes, unsmiling lips;
Yet these His brothers know not what they do.

And on his either side hang dead
A labourer and a factory hand,
Or one is maybe a lynched Jew

And one a Negro or a Red,
Coolie or Ethiopian, Irishman,
Spaniard or German democrat.

Behind his lolling head the sky
Glares like a fiery cataract
Red with the murders of two thousand years
Committed in His name and by
Crusaders, Christian warriors
Defending faith and property.

Amid the plain between His transfixed hands
Exuding darkness as indelible
As guilty stains, fanned by funeral
And lurid airs, besieged by drifting sands
And clefted landslides our about-to-be
Bombed and abandoned cities stand.

He who wept for Jerusalem
Now sees His prophecy extend
Across the greatest cities of the world,
A guilty panic reason cannot stem
Rising to raze them all as He foretold;
And He must watch this drama to the end.

Though often named, He is unknown
To the dark kingdoms at His feet
Where everything disparages His words
And each man bears the common guilt alone
And goes blindfolded to his fate
And fear and greed are sovereign lords

The turning point of history
Must come. Yet the complacent and the proud
And who exploit and kill may be denied –
Christ of Revolution and of poetry –
The resurrection and the life
Wrought by your spirit's blood

Involved in their own sophistry
The black priest and the upright man
Faced by subversive truth shall he struck dumb
Christ of Revolution and of poetry,
While the rejected and condemned become
Agents of the divine

Not from a monstrance silver-wrought
But from the tree of human pain
Redeem our sterile misery
Christ of Revolution and of poetry,
That man's long journey through the night
May not have been in vain

David Gascoyne

Father in Heaven! What is a man without Thee! What is all that he knows, vast accumulation though it be, but a chipped fragment if he does not know Thee! What is all his striving, could it even encompass a world, but a finished work if he does not know Thee: Thee the One, who art one thing and who art all! So may Thou give to the intellect, wisdom to comprehend that one thing; to the heart, sincerity to receive this understanding; to the will, purity that wills only one thing.

Soren Kierkegaard

Prayer

His agony can mount no higher.
He triumphs now, and cries out loud:
Father, take my soul
To you I commend my spirit,
Then he bows his head and dies.
His blood it is that has saved US from damnation;
For love of man he died the death of a sinner.
You gave us new life –
What can we give you?
We kneel at your feet, O Jesus,
deeply moved.
Accept our hearts as sacrifice.

Notes

All texts from the Bible are quoted from *The New English Bible* 1970 by permission of Oxford and Cambridge University Presses, except on page 30 where the version is Jerusalem.

So that the flow of the meditations would not be interrupted by citations, quotations in the text appeared without reference to sources. These sources are listed below in order of their appearance.

I

Masfield, John, 'Good Friday' from *Good Friday and Other Poems*.

Bonhoeffer, Dietrich, *The Cost of Discipleship*, trans R H Fuller, SCM, London, 1959, 76ff.

Bonhoeffer, *Letters and Papers from Prison*, trans R H Fuller, SCM, London, 1971, 348ff.

Berrigan, Daniel, *Consequences: Truth and ...*, Macmillan, New York, 1966, 31

The Prayer for each of the Seven Words is based on and adapted from a new translation by Sr Helen Butterworth of the texts used by Joseph Haydn in his choral version of the Seven Last Words of Our Lord on the Cross.

II

Dietrich Bonhoeffer, *The Cost of Discipleship*, 76

The inspiration for some of the ideas here derive from Samuel Parmar's *Lift Up Your Eyes*, CLS, Madras, 1975

Metz, J B and Moltmann, J., *Meditations on the Passion*, trans Edmund College, Paulist Press, New York, 1979, 8

Julian of Norwich, *Unfolded in Love*, DLT, London, 1980

Alabaster, William, 'Upon the Ensignes of Christes Crucifyinge', in H Gardner (ed), *The Metaphysical Poets*, Harmondsworth, Penguin, 1957, 44

III

Gunn, Thom, 'Jesus and His Mother' from *The Sense of Movement*, Faber and Faber, London, 1957

de Chardin, P Teilhard, *Pensées* no 19 in *Hymn of the Universe*, Collins, London, 1965, 92

IV

Bonhoeffer, *Letters and Papers from Prison*, 14

de Weil, Simone,*Waiting for God*, trans Emma Craufurd, Collins, London, 1951, 79ff.

Kierkegaard, Soren, *Journals* 1854, ed & trans A Dru, London, Collins 1958, 245

Kavanagh, Patrick, 'Having Confessed' in *Collected Poems*, Martin Brian and O'Keeffe, London, 1972, 149

Auden, W H, *For the Time Being*, Faber and Faber, London 1953, 65

V

John 4:4-8

John 4:13-14

St Bridget of Sweden, *Revelations*. Lib I, trans Weber, H R., *On a Friday Noon* , Geneva, WCC 1979, 18

Donne, John, *Complete Poetry and Selected Prose*, John Hayward (ed), Nonesuch Press, London, 1962, 285

VI

John 17

Muir, Edwin, 'The Killing' in *Collected Poems*, Faber and Faber, London, 1963, 224 ff.

Columban, *Epistola* VI/6, trans in GSM Walker (ed), *Sancti Columbani Opera*, Dublin Institute for Advanced Studies 1957

VII

Bonhoeffer, *The Cost of Discipleship* , p 77

Lawrence, D H., 'The Phoenix' in *The Complete Poems*, Heinemann, London, 1957

Yevgeny Yertushenko, *Almost at the End*, trs. Antonina Bouis, Albert Todd, and Yevgeny Yertushenko, Marion Boyars, London, 1987

Gascoyne, David, 'Ecce Homo' in *Collected Poems*, OUP, London, 1965

Kierkegaard, Soren, *Purity of Heart*, trans Douglas Steere, Collins, London, 1961, 27